POTLUCK

BY ANNE SHELBY
PICTURES BY IRENE TRIVAS

Orchard Books   New York

Text copyright © 1991 by Anne Shelby. Illustrations copyright © 1991 by Irene Trivas.
All rights reserved. No part of this book may be reproduced or transmitted in any form or by any
means, electronic or mechanical, including photocopying, recording or by any information storage
or retrieval system, without permission in writing from the Publisher.

Orchard Books, A division of Franklin Watts, Inc.
387 Park Avenue South, New York, NY 10016

Manufactured in the United States of America. Printed by General Offset Company, Inc.
Bound by Horowitz/Rae. Book design by Mina Greenstein.
The text of this book is set in 18 pt. ITC Quorum Medium.
The illustrations were painted in gouache, and are produced in full-color halftone.
2 4 6 8 10 9 7 5 3 1

Library of Congress Cataloging-in-Publication Data
Shelby, Anne. Potluck.
Summary: Alpha and Betty have a potluck and all their friends (Acton to Zelda) bring appropriate
alphabetical food (asparagus soup to zucchini casserole). [1. Food—Fiction. 2. Alphabet]
I. Trivas, Irene, ill. II. Title. PZ7.S542125Po 1991 [E] 90-7757
ISBN 0-531-05919-7   ISBN 0-531-08519-8 (lib.)

For Graham
A.S.

To Phyllis Perry
I.T.

Alpha and Betty
        decided to have a potluck. So—

they called up
their friends,

cleaned up their house,

and set their table—
for thirty-one.

Finally...

Acton appeared
with asparagus soup.

Ben brought bagels.

Christine
came
with
carrot cake
and
corn
on
the cob.

Don did dumplings.

Edmund entered with enchiladas,

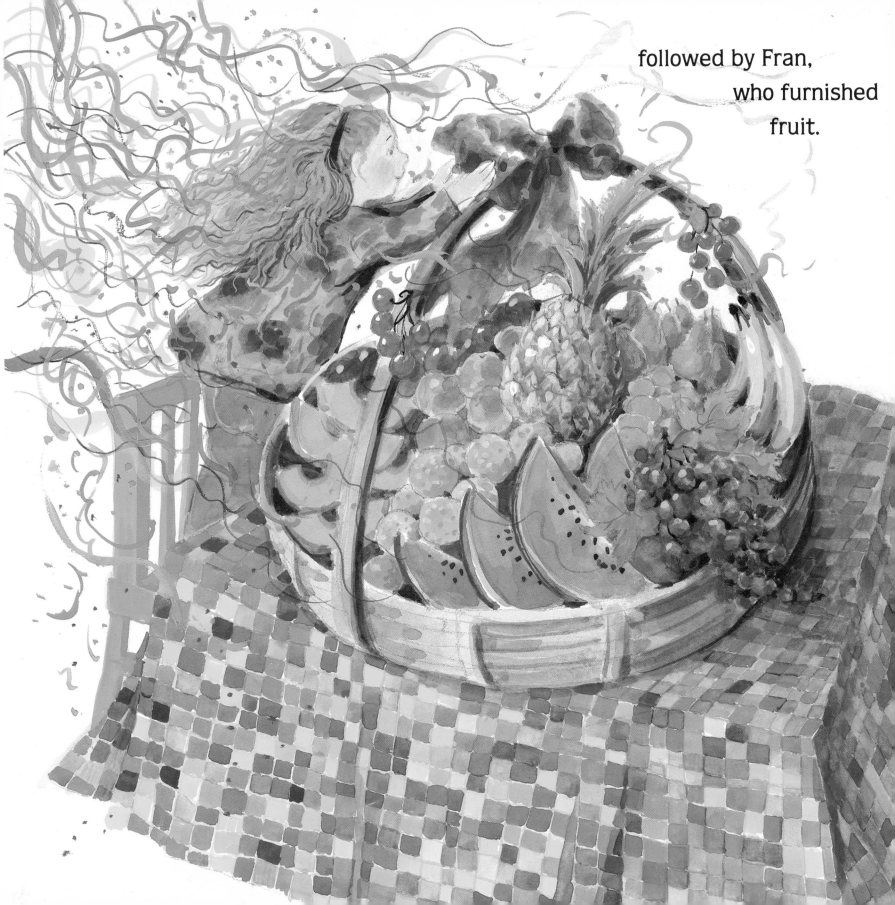

followed by Fran,
who furnished
fruit.

Graham had gone by Garbanzo's Bakery

to get good garlic bread.

H.B. had made
honey-sweetened hot tea.

Irene insisted on iced.

Kim with
a kettle of kale.

June joined in
with jelly rolls;

Lonnie loves lasagna,
  so he brought lots of that.

Monica made mounds and mounds
of mashed potatoes.

Norman knew that
oodles of noodles
would be needed.

Otis offered
onions;

Priscilla, a peanut-butter pie.

Quincy, of course,
brought quiche;

Rose,
her famous
rice and raisin
recipe.

Sam showed up with spaghetti sauce

subtly seasoned with spices.

The triplets turned up with tacos;

Ursula, with upside-down cake.

Victor ventured vegetarian stew,

while
Wally
wowed
the crowd

with his
wonderful
waffles.

Xavier
brought
some
excellent
examples
of
extra-special
X-shaped
cookies.

Yolanda
said yes
to yams
and yogurt.

But somebody was missing.

Who?

Then, at the last minute...

Zeke and Zelda
zoomed in
with zucchini
casserole.

So they all sat down
and ate
and ate and ate
and ate and ate.

They ate everything
from A to Z.